Light upon Light
- Poetry Collection -

Pinar Akdag

PINAR AKDAG

LIGHT UPON LIGHT

~ Poetry Collection ~

Impressum

Bibliographic Information of the German National Library:
The German National Library lists this publication in the German National
Bibliography; detailed bibliographic data are available on the Internet at
http://dnb.dnb.de.

2.Auflage
©2023 Pinar Akdag

Coverdesign, Buchsatz, Herstellung und Verlag:
BoD – Books on Demand, Norderstedt

ISBN: 978-3-7568-1015-4

This book is also available in German.

So greatly does that one now suffer in the night,
But over them light cautiously protects from fright.
Soon it will be all in the past, the nasty battle —
And you will wake up strong and bold.

Table of Contents

1. Poems from 2021

In the first section of this poetry collection, you will find interesting poems I, Pinar Akdag, have composed on current issues. I have had to overcome difficult circumstances in life and would like to share my experiences so that you, my dear friend, can benefit and be inspired.

Where are the miracles?

Thus speaks the atheist absent of meaning in this world:
"Pray tell where have all miracles in life been hurled?
Will mysteries, secrets just benefit
The fairy tales and legends, but no truth so requisite?"

So non-believers fail to see
The miracle they so would like in actuality.
This was to his chagrin and discontent,
So he persisted as a nihilist, and thus would vent.

The more the atheist persisted in his non-belief,
The tighter secret gates were locked for his relief
And joy in wondering, as he refused values pious,
Nor did he seek out faith or words of good in bias.

To witness miracles indeed,
We had to open up and recognize the need,
To seek the only truth, the one supremely sovereign,
You must believe in this – the great creator's reign.

However, if we close ourselves off to the light,
Our view and vision will turn life to utter blight.
No miracle will touch a single atheist,
His life was all in vain, eternity then speaks the words so salient.

Should he have had some faith in any good perfect,
This could suffice, may benefit him dead.

Let's light a candle in the dim and dark of night
To move along, to take that flight.

What would you tell the Creator?

Now may I dare to ask and hear you later:
What would you tell the Creator?
Could you not handle this prospect?
Might you recite a book direct?

Would you be wild, mad, annoyed or sad,
Would you not find words good, polite, to add?
Or did you want to tell it all, as we agree?
Then know this wisdom is unique for thee:

Don't you know that I often speak to Him,
And seek Him out to share my grief and all that's grim?
You too can do that, let me tell you,
Recline, relax, let it break through.

So share it all courageously in prayer.
Immerse yourself in perfect care.
Admit all your concerns, for better it will be,
He knows your pain, He rests in you, so as to see.

You'll feel it ease, be lighter in your chest,
He has so answered, helped you best,
To do, it is not hard and certainly not an art at all,
And now it's bright, an end to all the awful gall!

The lion and the treasure

The lions wander through the vast, imposing land,
Their treasure rests in dress invisible at hand,
Nature all shrouded in the earth and stone and sand,
Which hardly any animal had found upon demand.

Untouched are the great plains,
The animals all want to work, enjoying growing pains,
They want to work by day and rest at night,
They want to shout eternal longing to the heavens twilight!

They've run and struggled since the time before,
They search, explore now more and more,
The lions' treasure that they've scoured for,
May well leave them devoured.

But lions stride so forcefully,
Their secret's buried, there's no guide who'd bully,
Not one would dare dispute with them,
The kings who held the treasure gem.

Then it so happened that a horse rode up,
And eagle also dared to perch closeup.
They stared as silence reigned at first,
Until the horse spoke with a burst:

"Oh, lion, ruler with great power,
No, never have you lost in a tough hour.
We little animals beg you, ask you in our devotion:
Since time before, what is it that you lords regard as chosen?"

The lion kept his silence, waited for some time
To view the horse with kindness so benign.
The eagle clung to hope and spoke with clarity acute:
"All animals long for an answer, seek the truth."

The lion calm, deliberate, rejoined,
There was a power pure – eternal, light – within his voice:
"Do listen to my words and pay them heed –
For every treasure we, the lions, have stood guard.

We watch the treasure carefully and guide your lives,
It is too early still to gift that unto you besides.
But listen, all your lives, do not relent
In search of flawlessness that's quite evident.

It's they who seek shall find, an axiom always true each time,
We will help you in matters delicate and fine.
You should keep faith in God for good,
Prepare yourself for perfect life best understood.

If saints deem you worthy to land,
They'll lead you to the treasure at a rapid pace.
We may not lead you there, you must but understand,
Sincere ones find the secret place.

Now go your way safely in peace.
All faith can be the treasure, that's to say the least.
Your hearts and minds are the concern,
Avoid the night and don't succumb to what's forlorn.

And those of you who find the treasure soon,
They will find truths in noble form.
The treasure will make you a lion too –
So it echoes throughout the land affirmed:
A new ruler, a king, enters the world,
Embracing only inner wealth and never ever goods conferred."

World stage

The heroes walk lightly on earth,
They are active with no complaints henceforth.
They work in perfect harmony with life,
Never shall there be one defeat alone for your dislike.

They walk throughout the big, wide world,
There's nothing stopping their progress unfurled.
What do you think the world is in its fortress nation?
Is good then good, and bad so bad, who does the calculation?

Gray men are even scorned and feared,
Yet they too are heroes, though we like to judge here,
We think, we act now on our own,
Although it is not you, but they who guide alone.

Power is bad, and money even worse?
But no, here too is good or bad along with curses.
So only you see forcefully their strangeness wrought –
Up there is where the modern war is fought.

The good with power, bad with power –
Now everything they do so baffles us each hour –
But at some point, somewhere, who cares then what you are?
So whether day or night? For sure, it's not right near or far,
When you cause suffering, the world calls you then marred –
But look on earth at any time to stay abreast,
The angels weakened from the work do hardly rest,
Defend against attacks, protect the innocence of lives,
If you just watch, you won't see the next days.

Noble is man to not attack the others,
A lot depends upon protecting them and thy own neighbors.
The game of life is sensitive and may need strategy
So who directs desires, demands, possessions actually?

The world in many places is beyond control,
Peace does not come from words all closed, extolled,
It all needs everyone, and everyone needs everything,
So nothing needs no one, and no one needs nothing.

The Lord is everything; the Lord is but no one,
Mankind is all and nothing, that's in the long run.
Did you not always say so interspersed,
The world is only getting worse?
Our views exist as to the worlds among us,
Of import is that we are now victorious.
Just a few years ago, there was some pure reason,
There was the love and hope, our faith in some cohesion –
But hardly longer, as more people call for
Retaliation, hate, contempt, and so explore
For sparks of light, for something pure,
I say to you now and forever more of people,
All weakened here, they are mere sheeple,
The same old task she'd once gone in for,
She who discarded all she'd said before.

Are values trivial and vain?
Where is your faith, your light, where please explain?
Their worth, the people only prove to their existence,
To God, to their own selves, to all who come in presence,
Who do not listen to it all and everyone in pretense,
Who can preserve our common sense,
Who still realize what's good and right,
The ones who seek and find what's real and light,
Who struggle for the sake of humans,
And boldly fight for people's rights, a modest contribution,
While writing freedom on their flag no fury volley,
And who believe in brotherhood, with melancholy.

Who act and heal the wounds without arrest,
Who work away and never come to rest,
Those who then hope and pray and care
And wish blessings to people there.
Is there tomorrow for the people?
In such a way that's safe, without conditionals.

Fight for the good and know for sure,
The sovereign's ways are too obscure,
The one who went to create all with purpose and intent,
There is more than one way for all of us to frequent.

Be patient, persevere in battle for the light,
For giving up is not for you, nor may it ever be, alright?
Come now, let's light this candle
and down our path be sure to amble.

You there, me here, we'll fight so very hard,
To prove ourselves to us and everything that we regard,
Great shall be this here spectacle on earth in a short time,
The angels whispered that humanity shall turn sublime.

Light upon light

This life, we know what that is merely,
It's all so difficult and endless dreary,
Distressed we are, it is all bad, good gone
Whom did we do so wrong?

We look upon the ground – and lack all courage,
Don't see the stars and do not see our nature nourish,
We are not looking for the smiling eyes of children
And do not want belief in beautiful among our brethren.

Ugly is how we feel within our skin,
So many flaws we have, so no one takes us in.
Your eyes that dream there are so bright,
Nice fairy tales and legends from the light.

I look at you and so cheerful
You look down for a longer lull
Into abysses of this world so much,
You shout that you have no more hope as such

I will tell you that your today
Of all despair, and pain and suffering was yesterday,
What I lived through full force perpetually
And yet from night did I emerge eventually.
If you want to get out of suffering
Follow me and my humble words listening.
I want to give to you the means
So that you shine and laugh through life in beams.

Light upon light as you shall see,
So wait, now stand and witness, light will be.
I stood below, alone like you,
Come on, let's go, soon we can be all of it too.

Pearl
in the ocean

Like pearls in the great ocean deep
You are a treasure that does call for peace.
Don't seek the simple answer to the case,
But now escape this hellish place.

With every step you take ahead
The light should strengthen you and fill your head.
You'll be the candlelight in darkness long.
You shall go save the world, you will be strong.

You're like the sun, so full of light.
You are like love, eternal weight
In our existence, endlessly awake and given
Do not you think you'll be forgiven?

So hear me out: We all have obligations,
We all must work, assert ourselves in iterations
So ugly are some fights as known –
But yet: Your heart it calls us to be pure with God alone!

Look how you struggle with your destiny and cope,
You shout and shout, there is but no more hope.
And yet, misjudge the true value you hold,
You are worth more than all the worldly gold.

My soul embraces you who suffers all alone,
I am with you and tell you words to loan:
Search for the light and shine in teeming splendor,
So that the evil loses and you win, with the eternal power.

The world

Now look, dear friend upon the earth,
At how mankind descends the steps,
How they did hurt the world, the wounds so deep,
How they are lost in devastation, rage.

So listen, comrade dear in life's eternal story,
Did they then not have enough worry,
When they called loud to close their wanderings,
That they were looking to get help,
that courage was then fading?

Do you feel it, the pain and that discomfort,
Which they unto the world did give so long,
How they hurt earth and long did sleep,
Until life struck with fire, brimstone, embers back?

Please listen, breathe in deep and give your blessing pure,
Have courage, hope, kindness and love,
Until the sun comes out and laughs,
until appeased is nature called

And we respected these and tipped our hats.

Know that mankind is in the storm and rain,
Despair throughout. Where's patience gone?
We must redress the wounds in life
Before small efforts seem in vain.

No giving up can there now be,
We want to float to light because it's our Creator
Who gave us hope and will, so courage would not leave,
For faith, the good and peace should rest within us deep.

The wide land

Blessed is this land so vast, significant,
It is your home, from gracious hand magnificent,
Be proud of it, that is your good and vested right,
Do love your nation, you of noble might.

The same is true for every person good,
Proud figures they may reign across our global neighborhood,
Who walk and sow peace skillfully,
Yes, we are different – and but related so closely.

We're heading for great, gracious time,
Believe and work on all we cherish fine
So dream of better and more beautiful upon this world,
Look up and see you know you are a hero without sword

I take my hat off to yourself – majestic person,
Inside and out, you are ready so long ago, certain,
To heal the pretty, lovely land
In dress so glorious and grand

Is it so hard to be a governor of worth
One who goes out transforming all himself on earth?
No, you too can do it as well,
Come on, let's learn, let's do that something special.

I'll hold your hand and won't let go,
You're strong and great, as I've always known.
I pray for you day in day out, I am with you.
It's time to heal, the world's here too.

Now go ahead, embrace the light,
Because it's time for a new weight,
The world needs love, forget that not with any sight.
The night shall now give way, it's time and so let there be light.

In the garden

The garden bears abundant plants –
exotic flowers, vegetables and fruits.

The flowers shine to decorate –
carnations, lilies, roses, violets.

The senses celebrate the ornamental hedges,
shrubs, perennials,

Now cheer the fruit to pluck from trees –
plums and pears to pick with apples

And vegetables exude pure joy –
cucumbers, carrots and tomatoes.

So we go through the small idyllic paradise
as joyous recreation,

We even are quite modest in our observation,
As we don't want to make a change to this location,
At times like these, we want it all to stay as is, no mod'fication.

The garden should remain a splendid sight at any time,
We are not ready for departure of fall's fading vines.
We want it all to bloom forever, never seeing it snowing,
As lively celebration must in winter go missing.

You always want the smiling sun and light?
Remember this, please don't forget this sight:
When it is cold and awful out of doors,
You can still make it paradisical indoors

All snug and warm enwrapped in blanket fluffy,
A friend comes 'round the corner, proffering hot coffee,
You dive into books full of wisdom with a purpose,
Since you would like to learn and
ponder what's the point of us

The atmosphere so cool before the sun wakes up anew
And nature comes to life again,
bestowing joyful looks for you.

In summer we flanier outside, enjoying beauty in nature,
The garden tilled, ours is delightful culture.
We hike and walk and swim, embarking on one excellent tour
In winter we recede inward, read loads of captivating lit'rature,
We drink our tea, go bake and cook or clean,
this is the tried and true procedure.

So we accept with equal joy each season
As each does change, so start new things always for a reason,
It's not always cold and not always warm and there can always
Be something to enjoy, whatever phase.

Let us now try becoming optimists in life,
So then tomorrow will always teem with hope so rife.
Let's drop the quarrels and hate, let's learn forgiveness hence.
So till the garden, let us join in the experience,
How we do strive for one tomorrow shared with better sense.

The seasons they are warm and cool, we know
But this, for sure, is neither difficulty nor some woe,
We know the season's highs and lows,
Reminding us of lives, all possibility to grow,
Because our presence counts as well on earth below,

Enjoy your life, don't suffer such unrest
Do take a breath, no more distress.
You struggle way too much, now leave the stress behind,
Be patient, better it will be, so you won't mind

I wish some laughter bursting out, that's what for you to do,
Quite hard is life sometimes, this is a classic view,
We all know at some point freshly
The difficulty, it will come, and must be handled practically:
Just shrug your shoulders, shake off all the ugly,
Short suffer, if you must, Allah though
gave us struggle roughly

Defense is on our way,
So that you live the day carefree as you well may.

It sounds so easy when it's all behind and over,
Admittedly, however, most of this will be the same forever:
A harder skin evolved to complete you tougher,
So nothing then will end your way so quickly either.

Be sure to till your garden beds with diligence, vitality,
Enjoy the seasons with the peace, stability,
Walk with a heavy step, consider what is here at stake:
The suffering is relative, depends upon your inner state.
Time and again to suffer here is nothing but an awful plight,
So persevere with head held high and fight.

Change happens creepingly and gradually,
But then you get much stronger, many see it actually.
Those there must learn, it's common to be strong
in suffering here

You then gain strength and health, that is extremely clear.

Do not relent, I'll reinforce your injured back,
I will show you true bridges that you may now lack,
So that you can soon laugh again, and with delight
As you then pick the fragrant flowers when it's right

Eternal patience is important and
determination, my dear friend,

So far, adults have never shied
From dreaming, flying – nor have shown much regret.
Tomorrow it will all be better than is this,
There is no giving up – it simply does not actually exist.
Do not give up, for I believe in you above them all,
Tomorrow you'll be powerful, a joyful face on call,
No longer out of balance will you fall.

Now just hold out, relax and spare your nerves,
Until you gradually gain strength and will disarm, reverse,
The difficulty's scope will not control you like a curse.
Go out into the woods, the park, the meadow, garden lit,
Breathe deeply there, feel the fine wind so delicate.

Peace

On the vast land the peace doth rest
And nature shows its garment best.
The flowers, fragrance so intoxicate the senses here
You look about and stare, don't pause on where.

The sun it warms the source of light,
The rooftop sill, the blue sky bright,
Time-honored earth has been our faithful home immense,
However, it's the universe that holds the promise.

In life, we may much grieve from gloom –
Take heart, life, hope are blessings after doom.
Go search for paths, to all contributing
So like our bees and ants, we work when dancing.

We whirl around in rows to steady beats,
Our movements flow, no weight upon our flighty feet.
We are the day if comes the night,
Until appears the villain not.

If we then see sad eyes, we pat the shoulder:
"Head up, keep going, happy, cheerful!" we console her.
The storms, sometimes with thunder, will arise certainly,
But the Creator has directed us to toil effectively.

So let's go higher, higher up,
Keep going, going, to the top.
Surmount the circumstances,
With nature, peace we'll swift advance.

The morning dew

It's early in the rural valley underneath the blue.
The plants now drip with morning dew,
It has enveloped them, warm permeated so largely
It visits them for a short time, but very constantly.

Fine droplets of the early morning hour,
They give glad tidings of the dawn in all its power.
So cozy do they rest on plants much thicker –
It's quite a sweet and lovely picture.

No sooner does the sun gain strength by day
Than droplets go their way
To reach horizons with the power mild
Continuing the passion undefiled.

Splendor of colors

Blue is the sea and firmament,
This color is at any time present
That fills us any time of year to come
And gives consistency and freedom
The blue's refreshing and so soothing in the depths to plumb.

The green, by contrast, cheers the mighty nature,
It stands for freshness, health, with structure.
In ev'ry trace there is this balance,
It soothes and stimulates without a bit of malice,
Its harmony is pure relaxing, bliss.

For red is fire, and passion is for sure,
Its compromise is love and strength secure.
Pulsating vibes, seductive as they are,
Warm, hot, alive, and so bizarre,
Nevertheless turn dominant, likely to spar.

The color yellow is the gold and sun,
These two they steal our senses and then run.
The yellow is that love and cheerfulness,
Come optimism and lightness
And let the yellow play a role imbued with smartness.

With white, of course, we have the color purity,
It represents the innocence as well as clarity,
It signifies the light and just as much the lightness –
A color of tradition with much holiness.
It radiates a light for all eternity to us

And black's a number of its own,
It stands for night as well as sorrow.
At the same time it's also depth and winter.
Yet black is fascinating, sinister,
It's also elegant, a classic, modern, so chipper.

2. Poems from 2010

... This section contains poems by me, Pinar Akdag, that are over 10 years old and have not been published yet. They reveal my suffering at that time and my approach to solving the issues becomes clear.

I hope that these poems will inspire and help you.

Battle of day and night

Am I still worth the light of day?
Like swords that cut is each and every ray.
It's life they force on me,
I must believe it's good to be.

They show me splendor of the world,
For which the endless bloody battle's been unfurled.
They implore me and say the world is bright,
No matter deepest depths and highest heights.

Hardly so that it near beguiles me,
An intruder disturbs the picture of that happiness we see.
Inexorably, deep shadows grow quite inexact,
They bore and bite their way like rats.

And piece by piece destroy the color splendor,
Turn kingdom fairy tale into black night so dour.
Now conquered are the rays of sun,
They bicker, shout, were almost done.

They call to me, wait till tomorrow,
The black ahead, do not believe as we do follow.
We are the truth, they are the lie,
The night submits only to sun on nigh.

The whisper then intoxicating chokes,
Then chirping turns to croaks.
The Dark Empire stands supreme,
May be repulsive, but also a dream.

From every end and corner, they all stare at me,
Now they will try to turn me round to see
Well knowing that they didn't need it,
I do believe them, let me dive a bit,

Into the depths, into the nothingness, abyss,
Them understand and smile gently, as you speak the gist:

Do you see formless shadows inconspicuous?
Only the light makes them so pretty, so august.
See you the angular and frigid cold landscape?
For this, for dominance, humanity does scrape.

Does all that your eye sees have value now clearly?
No, but your people did desire that exactly.
Have pity on this world and all its endless suffering,
It will collapse quite soon, but no one has an inkling.

It's made of only rags, is covered with raw wounds,
Yet, no one can or will behold the dismal tombs.
Now realize human folly in its timelessness,
Enjoy the day by knowing where lies truthfulness.

Hiding

Surprised don't be at me, my gentlemen,
Don't hope they won't lock me away from them.
Because I've learned to hide myself as who I am,
Now you see me, your dream is gone in all the bedlam.

For after all they want a world of commonality and similarities,
For after all you fight the world of loneliness, profundities.

For them I am a nobody, no value and no meaning,
I am not needed, not an asset profiting.
My pockets are not filled, I have nothing of value,
Nor do I wear things noble, as you may like or as you do.

And I won't introduce my very self to you,
But will disguise it as your nobody but true.

I will continue with Allah and divine nature
And contemplating cities and their gray stature.
I will now live and you will hasten,
From bar to bar perpetually racing

I am in search of the true being,
They find themselves upon the trail of mere appearing.

I want to give instruction and admonish you,
Tell you what you do not suspect too.
You'll smile coolly and then nod wryly
And limp away from me embarrassedly.

I will look after you without much haste,
Don't think you've shaken me in such a case.
Formalities I have for you only,
Because these don't exist for me solely.

So stranger here, do tell me who you are,
Then I'll tell you just where you stand so far.
Your life's the world cold, hot, don't quit,
But look at who is keeping it.

The explanation

So far upon my personal trip, I've seen a lot of things,
Yet right just rarely did I get something.
The greatest was to find my faith,
Which then exposed my foolishness for my own sake.

I realized quick the multitude of my mistakes
And could not still preserve indifferent takes
Through this, and step by step, I moved ahead
Since then, day after day, I worked on it unbent.

It's true, you see, my body common like the others.
A woman plain and just as ordinary as all hers.
But I have tidied up my mind
And visit many distant lands and sites I find.

Through many worlds, I do now fly,
Discovering comfort and bliss thereby.
Because the world as true gives me not much,
It thinks only it's keeping me happy as such.

It me wants to amuse, and not much more,
But that doth give me nothing to adore.
Do not you see how all are looking round
And call for answers to abound?

Here, here, come here, I say then waving,
The world at large just wants to swallow you up flailing.
Take something of this truth for you
And thereby fill your empty pockets too.

The day the world at last does comprehend,
I'll let you know how I am doing on the way to face the end.
Then I'll grab you by your left shoulder blade anew
And prove the miracles of great Allah to you.

Big brother

Big brother, don't you recognize me?
Why in the world don't you protect me?
Why sadly do you look into my watchful eyes?
Do you not want to recognize my drive?

Both you and I, we know what's right,
The world at large, it is so bad, a blight.
Yes, brother, we do also know,
That good never gives up to go.

May be that we alone are simply way too minor,
To vanquish feats of evil once and then forever.
That you and I are not now heard,
That all swear innocence in every spoken word.

Big brother, you just watch, observe from on the pine.
And I am all alone, left suffering all the time.
Won't you come near to set me free,
Since we are in a lonely company?

I see, brother, you are not ready yet,
Nor do you see the time immoderate.
But brother, hear me out,
This ain't the forward route.

So after deep, dark nights,
And after many wins gained by the awful trite,
The morning must return and offer means to heal,
The light again may linger in the sky for real.

And, brother, I will seek just that, the light,
Because I don't allow madness to win the fight.

The course

The world will run its course
And it's not stopped by those events called worse.
Time passes without advertising,
It's this we see through aging.

Like rings around the tree,
Of space there's more and more we need
For all our thoughts and woes
And so let's hope for our tomorrow.

From early on we learn how to compete
So to prepare for life complete.
And step by step we learn to know and sense
And we have quite a clear conscience.

We let ourselves be steered and don't do any thinking
That these adults have monitored the things we're doing
For after all, we are the coming generation,
Now we are needed by the nation.

And first and foremost is to get an education,
No one has asked for your opinion.
This world of yours is your career
Amusement lags behind, far off there in the rear.

Should something else I say?
I hardly dare or may.
You do not have the time or energy
And aren't prepared to think or see.

To you I want to show a thing to shape the whole
And make a difference throughout, within your soul.
Indeed, there is a Lord,
And you should honor him one day in all accord.

That's all I ask of you lightly
And come a distance short with me.
Your Lord did you create,
Just as he did, your mind, one part of our nice fate

It's not just for your learning,
It is also in there for you to do reflecting.
So that you may find God,
Who loves so endlessly, no matter how you're odd.

Do they tell you that it has ceased now to exist?
So come and look upon my face in perfect bliss.
Can a coincidence achieve such an expression?
Your wall must soften soon, below the deconstruction.

So that you understand what is important then
And so that you are never left alone again.
Do learn, but go along with your beloved Lord,
In solitude, even, you will by him be honored.

He will protect and guide you
And tempt you into smiling too.
That you love him, you shall tell me,
Then I can say goodbye to thee.

... Then only, in the end, it's up to you, my dear,
Be your Creator there or here,
Whether you save yourself into eternity
Or live a short time here, and then so terminally.

The wanderers

Do you not see the ones, the souls who are now weakened?
Do you not hear the ones, the voices now quite frightened?
No way, you can't for sure.
Their countenance is not a bit more than a blur.

You see them walk the street,
They look so tough, the strongest bunch to meet.
As soon as all the doors are shut,
They all collapse like blisters cut.

There is a deep, black hole in them,
They need something, they know it then.
But search they never will,
They drink and fall upon their knees so ill.

The outcry of their soul suppressed,
They do not find the meaning, groping in the void depressed
If only I could 'proach them,
If only they would let themselves be helped right then.

They're caught within that vicious circle,
To tragic decadence they've turned upon referral.

Load

Time and again the organizer seeks your pack,
And puts a mountain on your back.
He doesn't like to see you as a floater oscillating,
But wants to crush and squeeze you to a dwarf thus pleasing.

Then as a corpse you creep and walk deathly,
So that your heart, your soul become so empty.
However, heart of stone, you now soften,
Don't give to him the victory, don't sink from being leaden.

Lean up, at last resist,
The word abandon is now gone, it is nowhere.
And if the load tries suffocation, please then do insist,
Believe in who you are, because for you someone's always
there.

Wish

What I for that would not but give
To see a different time and there to live.
In a completely different space
Than where was found my own birthplace?

Oh, I'm aware of it, this test,
To my great doubts it does attest.
Though somewhere else I might be better,
But everywhere there is deep water.

It may be brimming cockiness, yet you dive in.
And right away the tide ensconces you within.
So think and you will soon realize,
The immorality – it wants to reign and finalize

Right

Did you not always say so interspersed,
The world is only getting worse?
You were quite right, my friend,
With hatred streets are lined.

Angels

Are angels not afraid of us?
Because of us, are they not troubled to discuss?
Do they then think on earth we are the true devils,
The ones kept happy only by what's evil?

Deceptive silence

So silence you see me so long
And do not catch my heart in tears, no song.
You see I vaguely look below
And do not catch me drinking sorrow.

So call me what you like indeed
And see how wind now cradles fields.
Call me a chest, all full or empty
And look, there is much more to tempt thee
What I would like to share with you and tell,
I want your eyes to swell.

See how the day follows the night
And how we are well watched by sunlight?
See how the night follows the day
And this our peace nothing disturbs along the way?

Certainly, all this has meaning for the comprehending,
For those who're capable of hearing, seeing.
For they hear you, though they are listening not
And look at you, though they see not.
All this you want to bypass and give them their sense?
Do you not know that they are those
who don't forgive from thence?

So only stride towards them, try to save them from pain
Their hearts are locked and hang on chains.
As long as hearts of theirs don't soften,
You really can't achieve a thing often.

There is a piece of flesh in bodily complexity,
It is the most diverse way to achieve solidity.
If flesh is good, then man is good,
If it is bad, the blood of souls flows worse than should.
Know that this is your heart with power full,
It made a human turn an angel or a devil.

And see me 'waken, come to me,
For never shall from me be taken my own little sea.
Already I see busy life and the rat race,
Profundity and greatness do not have a place.

I am reluctant to return to that world crude
Which does not think much of a thought and search pursued.
So I do try to satisfy materialist life demands
And overhear because of my so dreamy nature reprimands.
To soften hearts as closed as these
It's with Allah's own help alone that it is possible
for you to now achieve.

One Look

The heaviness and black – they gnawed across my fronts,
And I then asked them what from me it is they want.
So I with weakened hands supported my own head,
I felt Allah, and it all would turn 'round, I said.

I gently rose and walked up to the covered window,
I pulled aside the curtain, gazed at a quite celestial show.
A living world revealed to me superiority
And gradually it let the night of my own body fade
away from me.

Astonished, I drew air with my mouth fully opened,
Absorbed the paintings so to sooth my wound deepened.
Gently I looked around, my face with a small smile,
Experienced amazed now that my feelings turn from trial.

It's daytime with bright light, I said unto myself,
Verily, with tribulation comes relief upon yourself.
I'm also trapped today due to my suffering way,
Salvation from my Lord is not a distant day.

Because I know, no one does suffer absent
some small interruptions,

Without you giving up the hope of your salvation.
So may the world decide opposed to you,
May it cause you nothing but pain and suffering too,
This heart would not give up this fight
And lean on its dear master all the time for knowing right.
My heart is fine
And I have that courage of mine
Have they then thought I would give up?
It's not like me to run amok.
Allah I love just so completely
And everything felt wonderfully.
Because if you can love Allah so too
Then nothing ever conquers you.
My soul now runs right to the light
And there's no stopping once the sight

Child of man

My child of man, let blessings be upon you,
You are what winds are into.
You roam the whole wide world,
You will not run into a halt.

My child of man, let blessings be upon you,
You are what ants are into.
You form such buildings fine
And do not let your grief be known this time.

My child of man, let blessings be upon you,
You are what mountains are into.
The earth so deftly you do hold
Be patient when you do as once you were then told.

My child of man, let blessings be upon you,
You are what mirrors are into.
In you, the world's reflected,
On you, time is refracted.

My child of man, let blessings be upon you,
You are what suns are into.
Within you rests a burning seed
And you arrange it all yourself indeed.

My child of man, let blessings be upon you,
You are what stars are into.
You are surrounded by your peers,
But nonetheless you will need just yourself as dear

My child of man, let blessings be upon you,
You are what none of others are into.
You are Allah's creation dearest
So finally prove it: Run to light to nest.

A song

Sing me a song of peace in this here place,
Please lift me up and wash the pain off of my face.
Do let me breathe again until I am brimming,
Because it's like all dreams are slipping.

I take a branch and lean upon it trustingly
And with it held tight in my grasp, I move ahead quite slowly.
The wind greets me, enveloping my body tight,
On pebble floor I have my name to write.

In depth do I regard my designation carefully,
The wind then comes and blows it out so quietly.
Quite unexpectedly I left this world behind,
The earth does not retain a single one of us in kind.

Thought I'd remain forever
And show my immortality to everyone to lever?
Just as the wind erased my name,
So am I next in line for death the same.

And in the time that I remain here,
Can I open my dreams a place to stay quite near
And bring them truth and make fulfilled
And sing my little song of will.

Die Autorin

Pinar Akdag wurde 1983 geboren, ist türkischer Herkunft und lebt in Bayern. Sie arbeitet als Autorin und Projektmanagerin. Seit ihrer frühen Kindheit las Pinar Akdag deutschsprachige Romane, Sachbücher und Klassiker sowie islamische Werke in türkischer Sprache. Dabei ging sie stets auch ihren Fragen über Gott und über die Welt nach. Stück für Stück sammelte sie Antworten und verinnerlichte diese - und hat bis heute nicht damit aufgehört, sich Fragen zu stellen und nach Wissen zu suchen.

Von einer frommen, engsichtigen Muslimin entwickelte sie sich so zu einer universell orientierten Person, die von allen Kulturen lernen will. Ihr Ziel ist es, schönes Wissen aus der islamischen Welt zu vermitteln und so diese fremde Kultur allen interessierten Menschen zugänglich zu machen.

Zugleich möchte Pinar Akdag für Frieden und Freiheit, Demokratie und Menschenrechte, Offenheit und Brüderlichkeit zwischen den Kulturen werben und dafür, dass alle voneinander lernen.

Pinar Akdag möchte Ihren Leserinnen und Lesern Wissen zugänglich machen, das sie inspiriert und vielleicht zu besseren Menschen macht. All jene auf der Welt, die sich für das Gute entscheiden, sind ihre Schwestern und Brüder.

KUVVET
SIEG ODER NIEDERLAGE

Manchmal ist der Kampf dein Schicksal

Lisa ist ein ganz normales Mädchen, als sie eines Tages Zutritt zur Welt der Schattenwesen erhält. Sie ahnt noch nicht, dass dies kein Zufall ist: Denn Lisa ist eine der Auserwählten, die nicht weniger als das Schicksal der Menschheit mitbestimmen wird. In einem Krieg zwischen Gut und Böse, in dem der Glaube der Schlüssel jeder Hoffnung ist, muss sie als Kuvvet, die Starke, als Gotteskriegerin gegen die Zweifel der Menschen und die Verführungen der Teufel kämpfen. Ihr Erzfeind Katros unternimmt unterdessen alles, um ihre Verbündeten, ihre Freunde und sie selbst zu vernichten. Die Situation, in der Kuvvet immer wieder selbst auf die Probe gestellt wird, wird immer auswegloser, die Niederlage scheint bereits besiegelt – wäre da nicht die Gewissheit, dass selbst der Untergang der Menschheit noch nicht das Ende ist … Ein epischer Kampf zwischen Gut und Böse in einer fantastischen Welt, die geprägt ist von der Mystik der arabischen Welt. Mit einer Protagonistin, die mutig und selbstbestimmt gegen die Hoffnungslosigkeit und für die Freiheit antritt.

Hardcover: 9783756853687 | 410 S. | 24,00 EUR
Paperback: 9783756866342| 410 S. | 12,99 EUR
eBook: 9783757831233 | 410 S. | 4,99 EUR